richard
sapper

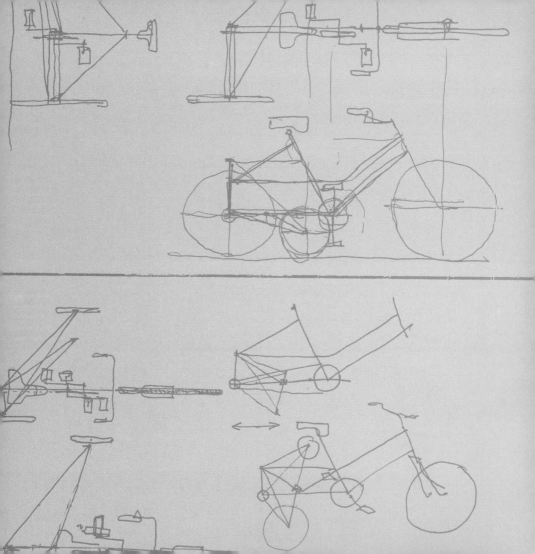

COMPACT DESIGN PORTFOLIO

richard
sapper

BY MICHAEL WEBB

EDITED BY MARISA BARTOLUCCI + RAUL CABRA

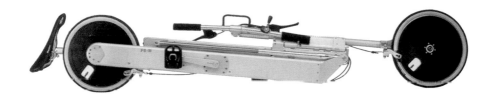

CHRONICLE BOOKS

SAN FRANCISCO

Foreword copyright © 2002
by Ingo Maurer.

Text copyright © 2002
by Michael Webb.

Design by Raul Cabra and Betty Ho
for Cabra Diseño, San Francisco.

Library of Congress Cataloging-
in-Publication Data available.

ISBN 0-8118-3282-1

Manufactured in China

Distributed in Canada
by Raincoast Books
9050 Shaughnessy Street
Vancouver, British Columbia V6P 6E5

10 9 8 7 6 5 4 3 2 1

Chronicle Books LLC
85 Second Street
San Francisco, California 94105
www.chroniclebooks.com

FRONT COVER: A GATHERING OF TIZIOS, 1972

BACK COVER: COBÁN ESPRESSO MACHINE FOR ALESSI, WITH STUDIES, 1997

PAGES 1 AND 3: PORTABLE AND COLLAPSIBLE ZOOMBIKE, 2000

PAGE 2: BICYCLE SKETCHES

FOLLOWING PAGE: MODEL OF ROBOT SOLDIERS, 1982

PAGE 8: ALGOL TELEVISION SET, DESIGNED WITH MARCO ZANUSO, FOR BRIONVEGA, 1962–64

NOTES

All quotations are from interviews conducted by the author, and comments submitted for this publication, except:

1. Gabriele Lueg: Richard Sapper, German-language catalogue of exhibition at the Museum für Angewandte Kunst, Cologne, Germany, 1993.

2. *Domus* 807 (June 1998; Milan).

3. Web site: www.Tizio.com.

4. *Domus* 807 (June 1998; Milan).

5. Richard Sapper, interview by Chee Pearlman, *New York Times*, 19 October 2000.

ACKNOWLEDGMENTS

Thanks to Ingo Maurer for so willingly providing the charming forward, and to Richard Sapper himself for being so generous with his time, memory, and photography archive. We also appreciate the celerity with which the people at Alessi and Magis provided images. Particular thanks go to Betty Ho at Cabra Diseño for her inspired eye and graphic talents, and to Chronicle's designer Vivien Sung, for trusting us aesthetically and encouraging our play. With regard to encouragement, where would we or this book be without our terrific editor at Chronicle, Alan Rapp, who early on championed the idea of this series? He was always at hand with sound editorial and design advice and good humor.

PHOTO CREDITS

Aldo Ballo, Milan
pp. 13 (chair and TV) , 26, 30, 31, 32, 33, 36, 37, 39 (all), 42, 43, 53, 54, 55, 64–65 (forks), 70, 73, 82, 85 (red TV), 86, 87 (all), 88 (all), 90, 91 (all)

Aldo Ballo for Alessi
pp. 58, 59, 61 (all), 62 (all), 64 (watch)

Artemide
p. 67 (drawing)

Boschetti reproduction
pp. 35, 56 (all), 71, 72, 76, 78, 79, 83

Riccardo Bianchi
p. 60

Serge Libiszewski, Milan
pp. 8, 34, 44, 67, 68–69, 77, 84, 85, 94

Knoll International
p. 41

IBM
pp. 20 (all) , 89 (all), 92 (all), 93

Magis
p. 38

Rheinisches Bildarchiv, Köln
pp. 6, 13 (radio), 24, 27, 28, 52, 66

Richard Sapper Archive
pp. 1, 2, 3, 13 (Sapper & Zanuso), 29, 48, 49, 50, 51, 63, 74 (all), 80

Ugo Mulas
p. 40 (all)

Unifor
pp. 54, 55

Roberto Zabban, Milan
pp. 46, 47

**Foreword by
Ingo Maurer**

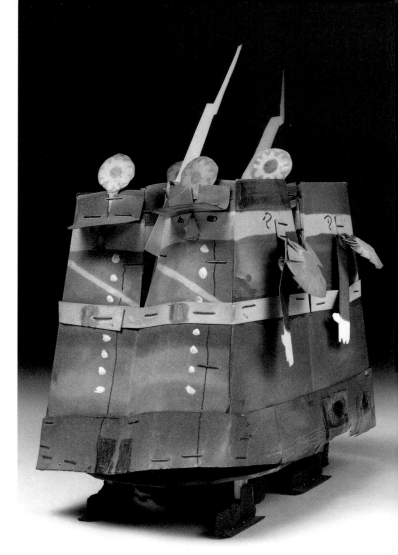

Thinking and writing about Richard Sapper, what comes first to my mind? He is strong; his *gestalt* is impressive. There is no aura of lightness or the slightest hint of frivolity. His eyes have the power of a Black & Decker drill. But this drill does not cause pain. When he looks at you, he gives you his full attention.

I have met very few persons of his caliber. Richard Sapper is a very *menschliche* (human) machine. He seems invulnerable, and in fact he is. That's part of his charm.

About six or seven years ago, he asked me to substitute for him while he was taking a sabbatical at Stuttgart's Staatliche Akademie der Schoenen Kuenste (a big mouthful, isn't it?). I was very surprised he asked me. Though we were born the same year (and are both designers) I consider him the exact opposite of me. However, we both share a love of refined *technic*. Working with his students, I understood him much better than before. They love and greatly respect him. Every year since 1993, the class has conducted a semester-long project called "Sapper's Rubber Cup." Participating students have to develop a vehicle with steered radio-control, using twenty-five grams of rubber for locomotion, with the goal of traveling as far as possible. Today's record is eight kilometers. The rubber can be stretched, bent, rolled—anything goes. The project produces a huge variety of crazy, technologically innovative lightweight machines. The cup races are big fun and have become legendary.

One of my own projects with Richard's students was to build a "Sapperlot" (an old-fashioned word for "slap me" or "upon my soul") that was based on his most famous work, the Tizio lamp. No, the project was not to build a lamp, but to design a machine, a sculpture, a fountain, or whatever with all the functions the Tizio has to offer, except light. Some of the results were hilarious. Richard's spirit was always there, though.

One of Richard's wisest decisions was his move to Italy. For all of us "heavy" Germans, a frivolous Italian provocation is good medicine. It has not hurt Richard's curious, wonderfully gifted love for *technic*. He is a great man.

Richard Sapper

Out of the Black Box   By Michael Webb

"Richard Sapper is a great designer," wrote graphics guru Paul Rand, "yet his work never shouts 'look who's here.' It has the appearance of a perfect flower with every petal in exactly the right place . . . He *always* begins with an idea—usually some mechanical invention—with German precision and Italian flair."[1]

Sapper's particular fusion of German and Italian cultures is evident in his most celebrated design, the Tizio lamp, as well as in the newly released Zoombike, a bicycle that can be folded and carried onto a bus as easily as an umbrella. In his versatility and sense of poetry, this prolific problem solver stands apart from his exact contemporary, Dieter Rams, the master of austere functionalism who helped make Braun, the appliance manufacturer, a powerhouse of postwar German design. He has also avoided the whimsy of movements like Memphis and the Italian preoccupation with style for style's sake.

Over the past forty-five years, Sapper has designed about 150 projects, alone or in collaboration with others. They include computers and clocks, timers and telephones, radios and television sets, experimental automobiles, folding furniture, and innovative espresso makers. Ten of them have won Italy's coveted design prize, the Compasso d'Oro, and nearly twenty have been selected for the permanent collection of New York's Museum of Modern Art (MoMA).

More Sapper works may be added to that pantheon, since Paola Antonelli, curator of architecture and design at MoMA, is a fan. "Besides being a great designer, he is a unique individual," she says. **"His warmth, enthusiasm, and generosity have not only brought us some of the most important icons of industrial design, but have also transported Modernism into a new phase by giving it fresh life."**

Like Charles and Ray Eames, Sapper is constantly searching for inventive solutions that surprise and delight users. Also like the Eameses, he despises the shoddy and ephemeral, and selects only those projects that excite him and those clients he finds congenial. Few other designers have worked for Mercedes-Benz as well as Alessi, for IBM *and* La Rinascente department store, satisfying corporations and consumers in equal measure.

Lean and lanky, with a hawk-like profile, penetrating eyes, and a fringe of silver hair, Sapper exudes an air of quiet authority. However, he feels no compulsion to design his own surroundings, and lives with his wife, Dorit—a former fashion designer—in a modestly furnished apartment across from the Castello in Milan. They also own an unpretentious house, high in the Hollywood Hills, which they love for its sweeping view and for the opportunity it gives them to visit with their son Mathias, who works in the movie business and lives in Los Angeles. Their two daughters studied architecture, but Carola now works as an investment banker and Cornelia creates computer software, both in London. Their reunions are rare, though, since Sapper is always dashing off to supervise an IBM design team or to consult with another client. When he is not in flight, he is likely to be juggling a dozen projects at different stages of development—some lasting weeks, others extending over years.

Born in Munich in 1932, Sapper grew up in the industrial city of Stuttgart. He returned to his native city to attend university, first studying engineering as an undergraduate, then philosophy and economics. While there, he became interested in design (the

Hochschule für Gestaltung at Ulm—a postwar version of the Bauhaus—had recently been established), but he wasn't sure it would make a suitable career. For advice he consulted his philosophy teacher. "He had a Venini vase on his table," Sapper recalls. "'Every time I look at it, it gives me pleasure,' he told me. 'So it is certainly a profession that gives people good sense. But to know whether you should dedicate your whole life to it, that is clearly something only you know within yourself.'"[2] It was all the encouragement Sapper needed. His father wasn't so convinced, however. Although he was a painter who felt strongly about the arts, he urged his son to take out insurance by completing his thesis on the economic problems of design. This pragmatic training would lead him to a job in the styling department of Mercedes-Benz.

"Back then, almost no one had a design degree, but we knew how to make things," Sapper recalls. "They say you can send a German into the jungle with a can of peas and he'll come out riding a locomotive."

In 1956, Mercedes still did things the old-fashioned way. Twenty people worked in a studio that was sandwiched between the assembly line and the offices, and management would occasionally stop by to see what they were doing. The doors had no handles; only the few with keys were permitted to enter. Sapper describes the review process: "To decide whether a car was beautiful involved only the chief stylist (who had learned his craft as a carriage maker), the managing director (who knew nothing about cars), the chief engineer (who was a genius), and their wives." No thought of focus groups or marketing consultants. One day, the sales manager protested to the chief engineer that the brakes shrieked—he could buy an American car with no such problem at half the price. The professor was unmoved. "We are using the best brake linings in the world," he replied. "If you can find better brakes that are quieter, we'll put them in. If not, not."

Sapper got his start at the company by redesigning a cone-shaped rearview mirror for the 300SL, and while he learned a lot in his two years at the factory, he was impatient to express himself. "I wanted my freedom and understood I was not the type to work within a big corporation," Sapper explains. He went on to land a job at Gio Ponti's architectural studio in Milan, just as construction was starting on Ponti's masterwork, the Pirelli tower. "Those first years in Italy were the most wonderful of my life," Sapper recalls. "The studio had forty young people from all over the world. It was creative chaos. Italy was in the middle of an economic boom. All you needed was an idea—anything was possible. The city was full of enterprising people who were interested in culture and design, and almost everything they touched turned to gold. In-cre-di-ble!"

His first independent success was also serendipitous. After leaving Ponti and joining the design department of La Rinascente, he took a call from a businessman who badly wanted to win the Compasso d'Oro for a clock that would use up his stock of war-surplus torpedo timers. For Sapper, the clockwork mechanism was his "can of peas." He enclosed the timer in a steel tube and added a weighted, self-righting, round base that contained a battery. The face was a copy of one from an airplane pilot's clock he found in a flea market. The marriage of the exaggeratedly bold numerals with the sleek casing helped him carry off the prize. Lorenz's Static table clock, considered revolutionary on its first appearance in 1959, launched Sapper's career. It is still in production.

Marco Zanuso, who was already well established in Milan as an architect and designer, invited Sapper to help develop products, and they collaborated, on and off, for about fifteen years, until they discovered that most clients didn't want to pay for two designers. During their association, they created a succession of television sets and other consumer electronics for Brionvega, sewing machines for Necchi, and the Lambda sheet steel chair for Gavina. "Marco and I thought in different ways—but we had a wonderful dialogue and something interesting usually came out of it," says Sapper. "He has a very strong artistic element in his thinking, and I have a very strong technical/practical feeling. I'm always reflecting about the structure and how it should work and move. Zanuso was concerned more about the form. Put them together and you have what you need. I've learned a tremendous amount from him."

The list of their joint projects is surprisingly eclectic, ranging from an olive oil centrifuge to a wooden school desk and an Alfa Romeo sports car. Standouts include the

wonderfully chunky yet lightweight K1340 children's stacking chair for Kartell, which looks as though a child had provided the concept sketch. **For Siemens they designed the Grillo, the first one-piece telephone, with a flip-down mouthpiece, a design that anticipated the current generation of cellular phones. The TS-502 radio has a bright red plastic container that hinges open to reveal the dials and speakers.** In contrast, the Black television set, also designed for Brionvega, is a hard plastic cube that is as impassive and sharp-edged as the monolith in Stanley Kubrick's *2001: A Space Odyssey.* In the real year 2001, it has become a fetish object as exciting to urban sophisticates as the movie's monolith was to the apes.

It was Zanuso's idea to hinge the radio, but the folded object would become a recurring theme in Sapper's work. His Plico tea trolley and Nina chair fold flat to save space and make for easy carrying. Collapsibility is also what makes his Zoombike so handy and appealing. However, with the Grillo and the TS-502, the motive is surprise: turning a plain container into an intriguing and useful object. Sapper describes the IBM ThinkPad as a cigar box that you open up to reveal something entirely unexpected. This laptop began as a slimmed-down version of the black box, another idea to which the designer often returns.

In an era of computer-generated blobs and squishy, multicolored, "user-friendly" shapes, Sapper swims against the tide. He finds a timeless beauty in minimal, monochromatic, orthogonal forms. It is his invisible signature, one that adds value to the product. More than ten million ThinkPads have been sold, and research has determined that up to a third were chosen primarily for their appearance. A top New York law firm uses brand X computers in the office, but sends its attorneys to court with ThinkPads to intimidate the opposition. The casing has changed little in eight years, even though the contents are upgraded every six months or so.

Rigorous as he is, Sapper enjoys a joke. In a 1981 Berlin workshop organized by Alessi with Ettore Sottsass, he came up with a spaghetti fork that is as frivolous in its shape, colors, and function as anything by Memphis. When used according to instructions, it sprays sauce over you and your neighbors— a delightful triumph of dysfunctional design.

Throughout his productive collaboration with Zanuso, Sapper continued to work independently. "If I had accepted everything, I would have had a big office," he says. "I've kept my independence while working for some of the largest corporations." In 1971, an offer he couldn't refuse came from Ernesto Gismondi, an aeronautical engineer who founded the Milan-based Artemide lighting company forty years ago. Gismondi is famous for treating his favorite designers like family, challenging them in turn to solve specific problems. In Sapper's case, he asked him to improve upon the work lamp, and the designer agreed because he needed one himself.

The concept of the Tizio came quickly. "I prefer having the light shine on just the piece of paper when I work or read," Sapper explains. "It's necessary to position the reflector fairly close to the paper. If it's too large, it turns into a rather disturbing object close to the head. And I wanted a work lamp with a wide range of movement that would claim only a small amount of space."[3] He sketched a weighted transformer base and counterweighted arms conducting low-voltage current to eliminate the wires and springs that characterized adjustable desk lamps like the Anglepoise. However, the ball joints he originally chose allowed the arms to sag. What was needed were joints with more friction to hold a steady position. He discovered that press-studs would do the job and would snap apart rather than break if the lamp was dropped. By happy chance, the halogen bulb was introduced during this process. Sapper substituted a 50W halogen for two small incandescent bulbs, enabling him to reduce the size of the head. He showed the prototype to Gismondi, who exclaimed: "Jesus Christ! We'll make it!" The Tizio is nearly thirty years old, and some 1,500,000 have been sold. The basic design has changed little, but Sapper is disappointed that the swivel-headed Super Tizio, which he developed a few years later, has not supplanted it.

The 1970s were a productive decade for Sapper. Alessi commissioned the Caffetiera 9090, a stove-top espresso maker that is durable and elegant. Knoll, the American manufacturer of contemporary furniture, gave Sapper's name to a handsome group of office chairs he designed. He also created a succession of clocks and timing devices. Much of his time, however, was devoted to transportation issues. He worked with Fiat on experimental cars, developing features that could be incorporated into current production models. One of these was a sophisticated pneumatic bumper—a kind of external air bag—that would cushion the body from a 10 mph impact. It was conceived as a response to a new U.S. regulation mandating such safety devices, but Detroit's lobbyists had the rule overturned. That eliminated the motivation for Fiat, which installed a cheaper plastic bumper on its new automobiles.

Another project launched Sapper's often frustrating quest to develop portable personal transportation, sparked largely by his encounters with the chaotic traffic in Milan and other congested cities. In 1972, Sapper collaborated with Gae Aulenti in a competition for alternatives to the automobile, exhibiting their proposals for bike tracks and moving walkways at the Milan Triennale. The display included the prototype of a transparent bicycle umbrella that would protect the rider from the city's frequent rain showers. **Sapper designed a bus for Fiat that enabled passengers to stow their machines in a rack located below an elevated driver's seat, but the company determined that few transit authorities would give up the buses they had to adopt it.** He developed a folding steel bicycle with small wheels for Batavus in the Netherlands—that nation contains the highest concentration of riders outside of Asia—but it proved too heavy to carry far. And the experimental folding scooter he presented at the 1979 Triennale was judged too slow to challenge the bicycle. Ironically, today, inexpensive, low-tech scooters are all the rage. Sapper, as always, was searching for a more sophisticated solution.

Over the next two decades, he designed fifty prototypes for a folding bicycle before he felt he had it right. The challenge was immense. "A bicycle is a wonderful machine," says Sapper. "The proof of that is that it has hardly changed in a hundred years. It took off with Dunlop's invention of the pneumatic tire, which cushioned the rider without consuming energy. It was invented as a substitute for a horse. And not only is it smaller, lighter, and easier to store than a horse, it also doesn't need to be fed. However, if you compare it to an umbrella, it is extremely cumbersome—it requires a rack on a car, and it is not easy to put it in an apartment. I wanted to invent a bicycle that had all the conventional features, but could be folded as quickly as an umbrella, and would be small enough to fit in the trunk of car or a closet at home. I thought: What if the bicycle had not been invented, and I could design one with the same advanced technology as an aircraft's landing gear? I tried it and found I could."

Someone once asked Charles Eames if the design for his molded plywood chair had come in a flash. "Yes—kind of a thirty-year flash," he replied. Sapper could say the same of the Zoombike, which went into production in 2000. He has rethought every part of the structure, selecting different metals to achieve an ideal mix of lightness and strength, and reducing dimensions while accommodating the human frame. The model that Elettromontaggi has begun to produce in Italy has three gears, speedy acceleration, and the maneuverability one needs on the narrow streets of European cities. However, in the United States this brilliant invention may have a harder time winning wide acceptance. Few American urban dwellers commute to work by bike. And it's the poor who typically most need personal transport at either end of a bus or train journey. But the Zoombike is precision equipment with 550 separate parts and an estimated retail price of $1,500. Perhaps skyrocketing fuel prices will change commuting patterns, finally persuading the affluent to leave their cars at home.

In many ways, the Zoombike is a paradigm of its inventor. Sapper travels light, employing expert assistants, often former students, only as needed, and he generally deals with companies on a project-by-project basis. Even complex jobs are executed by a tight crew, since, as he notes, "when the development team is bigger you encounter too many obstacles." He still prefers to model his designs in three dimensions and to use computers only for structural analysis or to generate working drawings. **"I do not think it is possible to analyze a problem exhaustively—rather, I trust intuition," he explains.** "With a brilliant idea you can solve a problem but you have to refine it to make it practical. You make a sketch or model to give form to the idea, but it doesn't come alive until it is injected into the larger world of a company or a factory. Many other people have to have a dialogue with you and make a product out of it. As a result, the model changes—sometimes for the worse, sometimes the better."

Commissions and self-generated projects both demand the same high standard of execution. "Experience has taught me that there are very few industrial companies with whom you can do good productive work, of the quality I want to achieve," declares Sapper. "It is possible to work with even the biggest companies, but only if there is a director interested in beautiful things. The attraction to beauty is so strong that no one can beat it. If, on the other hand, you get a client who understands nothing about aesthetics, then you've wasted your time." To illustrate this, he told an editor of *Domus* magazine about a revolutionary ship he designed for an Italo-American joint venture. Everything went smoothly up to the final presentation, when the door opened and in came the American partner. "I saw the watch on his wrist and I knew I had done all that work for nothing," he recalls sadly.[4]

Sapper is characteristically outspoken on the issue of sustainability. "I am a great enemy of planned obsolescence," he declares. "Producing a product so that it will break down and you will have to buy a new one is criminal."[5] However, he insists there are no easy answers. "Responsibility toward the environment is plain commonsense; you use recyclable materials whenever you can—no need to go off and talk about it," he says.

"Too often people do lousy designs and try to justify them in the name of ecology. Virtually everything in a car can be recycled if you label the materials. Plastics are usually easy to recycle and require less power to produce than aluminum, for example.

"It's not a simple issue," he insists. "With a laptop computer, you try to balance conflicting factors—of weight, rigidity, thinness, magnetic shielding, heat absorption, and production cost. I once used plastics reinforced with carbon fiber, which cannot be recycled, and is expensive and fragile—but very light, and therefore appealing to the customer and less expensive to ship. You can save a pound and pump up the cost by demanding more sophisticated and expensive contents. I try to use materials that are cost-effective—but that can be calculated in different ways. For instance, I collaborated with Alan Fletcher of Pentagram in London to design plain brown packaging with relief typography for Federal Express. But they rejected it."

Sapper's largest, most enduring client is IBM, whose former CEO, Thomas Watson Jr., declared that "Good design is good business." Since 1980 he has occupied the position of corporate industrial design consultant, in succession to the fabled Eliot Noyes. His role is to work with management to establish an overall design strategy and to oversee design for IBM worldwide. Additionally, he creates key products in collaboration with specialized teams in Raleigh, North Carolina; Rochester, Minnesota; Yamato, Japan; and a fluctuating number of satellite studios.

In the 1980s, Sapper felt frustrated by the size and diversity of IBM. Buoyed by record profits, the corporation went in too many directions at once, producing a jumble of products and losing both its focus and its profitability by the end of the decade. Sapper helped steer the company back on course, returning to Noyes's concept of using design to create a contemporary, unified image. As David Hill, IBM's director of personal systems group design, explains: "Richard is a teacher, leader, catalyst, and collaborator.

His approach to design is very purposeful and intelligent, and the ideas he comes up with are easily translated from one product to another. He visits the major centers as often as six times a year, and these are hands-on sketching sessions. It's a team effort—collaborative, open, and creative. Santa's elves stay up all night making changes. Next morning, we may say, 'This doesn't work,' or 'This needs more work.' Richard gets out his scissors, pieces of paper, and scotch tape. Next thing you know, we've got a great design.'"

The ThinkPad, which made its debut in 1993, was a breakthrough—for its innovative design, brilliant screen, and sleek 10-by-13-by-1 inch container. It is a symbol of power that can be slipped into a Mark Cross portfolio—justifying the premium price and the need to plug in peripherals. Sapper fought to make it black—a major departure from IBM's customary pearl white and a first in the industry. Once adopted, it became part of the rejuvenated IBM image. As Hill points out, black makes screens appear brighter and cases slimmer, and the color is as timeless and universally acceptable as a Steinway grand.

"Computers were boring for a long time, but they are now becoming exciting," Sapper observes. "Getting IBM to change its thinking was like turning a supertanker. I am trying to alter the idea people have of a PC to let it become something else. Because I think people are sick of those boxes."

The designers were on his side. Hill challenged his team at Raleigh to break out of the box by rearranging the components and exploiting flat panel displays and other improved technologies. An early experiment was nicknamed "Stealth" for its resemblance to the F117A fighter.

Stealth is an apt moniker for the NetVista X40 desktop computer, which Sapper and his team developed in only two and a half years; it was released in mid-2000. The concept is to hide the computer and allow users to concentrate on what it does for them. Most of the circuitry is concealed behind the flat fifteen-inch screen, and the rest is housed in a compact six-inch-square base. Drives drop down from the slender neck that links the two. As an object, it is the best-looking PC to date. But its elegance is compromised by the tangle of cords required to link it to an external zip drive and modem (neither made by IBM), without which the machine is unable to back up files from the hard drive or handle DSL. However, as with the ThinkPad, the design provides a solid foundation on which to build, allowing designers to integrate new features as they become more compact, and substituting wireless connections to the keyboard, mouse, and peripherals. The X40 may become the Porsche 911 of the computer world.

Fierce competition and the accelerating pace of technological change spur IBM to develop even more innovative solutions. Already, the IF 2000 radial arm allows a flat panel to rotate in every direction, much like the Super Tizio; wires and processor are concealed beneath the work surface. Currently under development is the Wearable PC, a handheld, battery-powered translucent box with the power of a ThinkPad that weighs only 10.5 ounces and has an eyepiece that turns chip-sized displays into images appearing to be twelve inches across.

It is a huge leap from the refined, quality-obsessed designs of a blue-chip corporation to the messiness of the world outside. Sapper blames advertising and the press for the pervasive ugliness of so much of what surrounds us. "When everything is acclaimed as new and fabulous, designers have to find something else to put on a pedestal three weeks later," he laments. "Good design was always rare, but bad design was nameless—it was bad because nobody cared about it. Now there's a lot of famous bad design, involving huge amounts of time and effort. When I was young, most people didn't know what a designer was—only those manufacturers who wanted nice products out of a desire for quality and prestige. Mercedes knew better than anyone else that they made the best-looking cars. Today, in many corporations, design decisions are in the hands of people without the slightest knowledge of the subject, asking consumers what they want."

His eyebrows bristle as he warms to his theme. **"Jogging shoes are a truly ghastly product, and Swatch's Smart has to be the ugliest automobile ever designed. Marketing people no longer sit side by side with the designers—they sit on top of them."**

Nobody is sitting on top of Richard Sapper, and if they tried, they'd soon be unseated. He is a lone eagle, self-taught and self-propelled. A master of the black box, he is in no way imprisoned by it. Though proud of the Tizio and other classics, he looks forward, not back. In 1997, he designed the Aida, a cheap and cheerful stacking chair with a stamped-out colored plastic shell supported by a single piece of bent metal tubing. There are no screws and nothing is welded; the two parts are simply threaded together. A year was spent rethinking the electric espresso maker, resulting in the Cobán, a precision machine manufactured in Switzerland and marketed in three versions by Alessi. To a greater degree than rival products, it clearly expresses its function: a transparent dome-like reservoir of water supplies an engine that forces steam through the finely ground beans. It allows the user to make as intense a thimbleful of espresso as one would get in the best Italian bar, without real effort, yet it invites interaction. That seamless, enjoyable interaction between object and user is for Sapper one definition of a design classic.

The Cobán is named for a little town in Guatemala where Sapper's grandfather grew coffee. His father was born there, and after moving to Munich, he continued to receive regular shipments of coffee beans from the plantation. So this machine has personal meaning to the designer. So too does the jewelry he created exclusively for his wife. To please one of his daughters, who was then running a gelateria in Pasadena, Sapper entered a newspaper competition in Germany, shaping an ice-cream cake in the guise of the Titanic. However, these are momentary diversions from his relentless pursuit of perfection.

Sapper's current work roster includes more products for IBM, Alessi, Alfa Romeo, and Fiat. In the meantime, he dreams of the hundreds of things he hasn't yet designed, including a combine harvester. And he looks forward to avoiding the traffic in Milan by traveling through the streets on his Zoombike, and then folding it up and carrying it onto the subway on his way home. German efficiency in the capital of Italian design.

Sapper got his start at Mercedes-Benz by redesigning a cone-shaped rearview mirror for the 300SL. Although he learned a lot in his two years there, he was impatient to express himself. He went on to land a job at Gio Ponti's architectural studio in Milan.

REARVIEW MIRROR FOR THE MERCEDES-BENZ
300SL ROADSTER, 1956

MINI TIMER FOR TERRAILLON, 1971

ESCARGOT KITCHEN TIMER FOR TERRAILLON,
1980

HELIOS WALL CLOCK FOR LORENZ, 1970

SANDWICH CLOCK FOR RITZ-ITALORA, 1971

STATIC TABLE CLOCK FOR LORENZ, 1960   TANTALO CLOCKS FOR ARTEMIDE, 1971

Sapper took a call from a businessman who badly wanted to win the Compasso d'Oro for a clock that would use up his stock of war-surplus torpedo timers. He enclosed the timer in a steel tube and added a weighted, self-righting, round base. The face replicated an airplane pilot's clock. By marrying the exaggeratedly bold numerals to the sleek casing, Sapper carried off the prize. Lorenz's Static table clock, considered revolutionary on its first appearance, launched Sapper's career. It is still in production.

MATCH TRANSISTOR RADIO FOR TELEFUNKEN,
1962

TRANSMASTER 7 TRANSISTOR RADIO FOR
LA RINASCENTE, 1958

KNIFE SHARPENER FOR NECCHI, 1964

NECCHI 564 SEWING MACHINE, 1971

HAIR DRYER FOR LA RINASCENTE, 1958

AIDA STACKING CHAIR FOR MAGIS, 1999

K1340 CHILD'S CHAIR, DESIGNED WITH
MARCO ZANUSO, FOR KARTELL, 1964

LAMBDA CHAIR, DESIGNED
WITH MARCO ZANUSO, FOR
GAVINA, 1963

EXECUTIVE ARMCHAIR FOR KNOLL, 1979

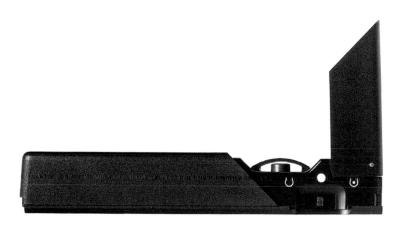

MICROSPLIT 520 STOPWATCH FOR HEUER, 1976

During the years Sapper and Zanuso collaborated, they created a succession of television sets and other consumer electronics. It was Zanuso's idea to hinge the radio, but the folded object would become a recurring theme in Sapper's work.

TS-502 TRANSISTOR RADIO, DESIGNED WITH
MARCO ZANUSO, FOR BRIONVEGA, 1965

GRILLO TELEPHONE, DESIGNED WITH
MARCO ZANUSO, FOR SIEMENS, 1965

FOLLOWING PAGES: RICHARD SAPPER AND
MARCO ZANUSO WITH THE GRILLO PHONE IN 1965,
AND WITH THE TS-502 TRANSISTOR RADIO IN 1991

PLICO COLLAPSIBLE TEA TROLLEY
FOR BILUMEN, 1977

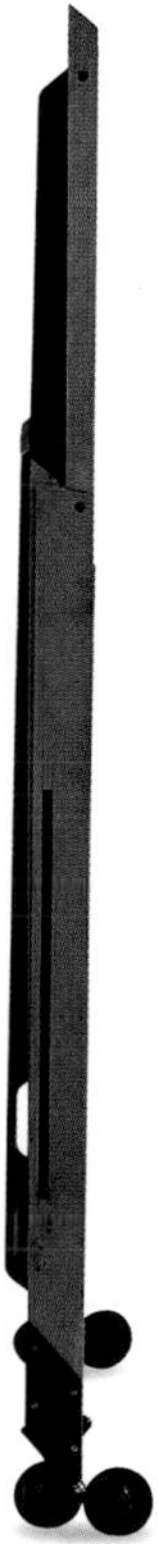

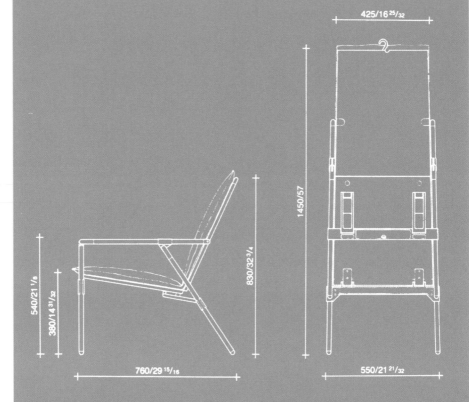

425/16 ²⁵/₃₂

1450/57

830/32 ³/₄

540/21 ¹/₈

380/14 ³¹/₃₂

760/29 ¹⁵/₁₆

550/21 ²¹/₃₂

NENA FOLDING ARMCHAIR FOR B&B ITALIA, 1984

CABINET SECRETARY FOR UNIFOR, 1988–89

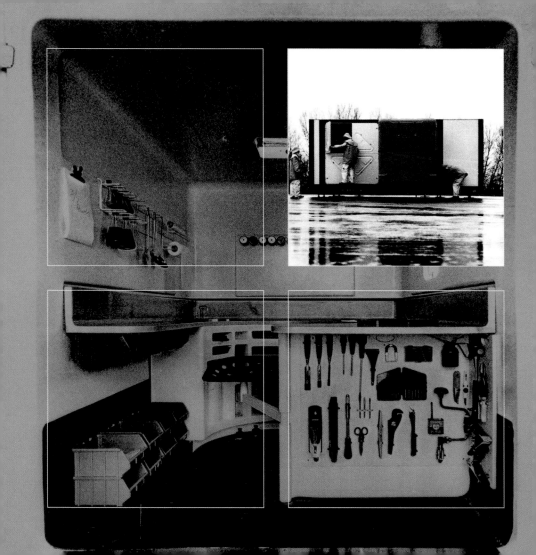

It is a huge leap from the refined, quality-obsessed designs of a blue-chip corporation to the messiness of the world outside. Sapper blames advertising and the press for the pervasive ugliness of so much of what surrounds us. "When everything is acclaimed as new and fabulous, designers have to find something else to put on a pedestal three weeks later," he laments. "Good design was always rare, but bad design was nameless."

PROTOTYPE FOR LIVING CONTAINER, DESIGNED
WITH MARCO ZANUSO, 1972

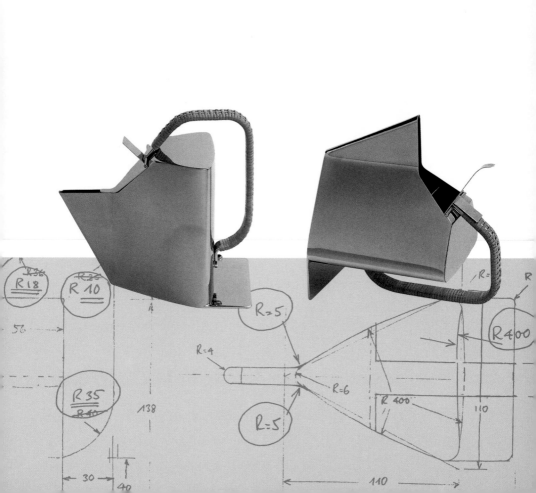

BANDUNG TEAPOT FOR ALESSI, 1990

TWO-NOTE WHISTLING TEA KETTLE FOR ALESSI,
1984

COBÁN ESPRESSO MACHINE FOR ALESSI
WITH STUDIES, 1997

9090 ESPRESSO MACHINE FOR ALESSI, 1978

CINTURA DI ORIONE COOKWARE
FOR ALESSI, 1986

RS01 CUTLERY FOR ALESSI, 1990

FAR LEFT: HASTIL FOUNTAIN PEN, DESIGNED
WITH MARCO ZANUSO, FOR AURORA, 1972

MIDDLE LEFT: URI URI WRISTWATCH FOR
OFFICINA ALESSI, 1988

LEFT AND RIGHT: PROTOTYPE SPAGHETTI FORK
WITH SPINNING MECHANISM FOR SPLATTERING
SAUCE, 1981

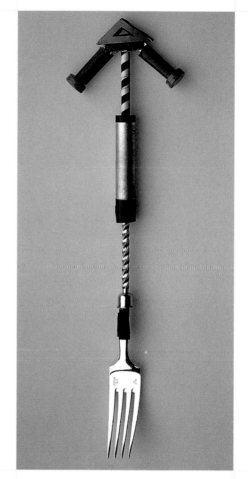

"I wanted a work lamp with a wide range of movement that would claim only a small amount of space," says Sapper about his design of the Tizio. He sketched a weighted transformer base and counterweighted arms conducting low-voltage current to eliminate the wires and springs that characterized adjustable desk lamps like the Anglepoise. He showed the prototype to the head of Artemide, who exclaimed: "Jesus Christ! We'll make it!" It would become a best-selling design icon.

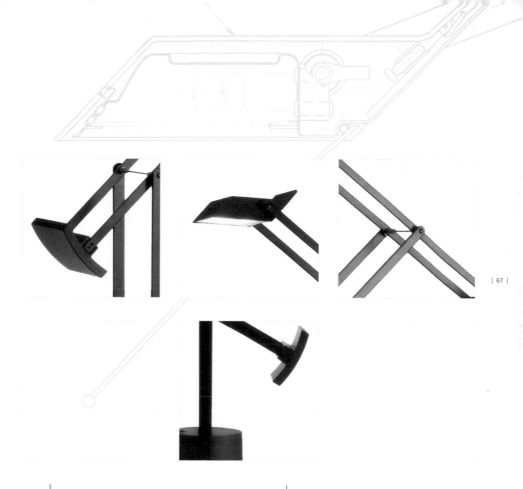

LEFT: STUDIES FOR TIZIO LAMP, 1970
ABOVE: DETAIL ELEMENTS OF TIZIO LAMP

FOLLOWING PAGES: TIZIO LAMP FOR ARTEMIDE, 1972

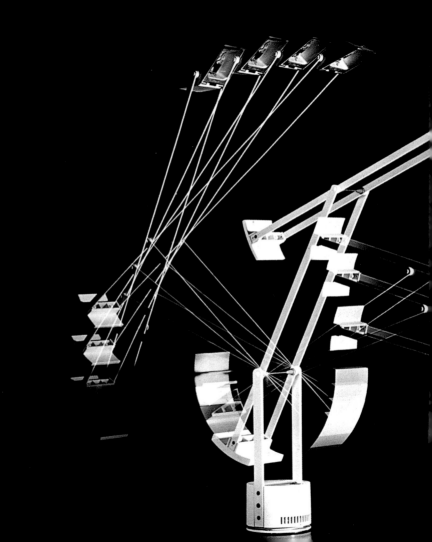

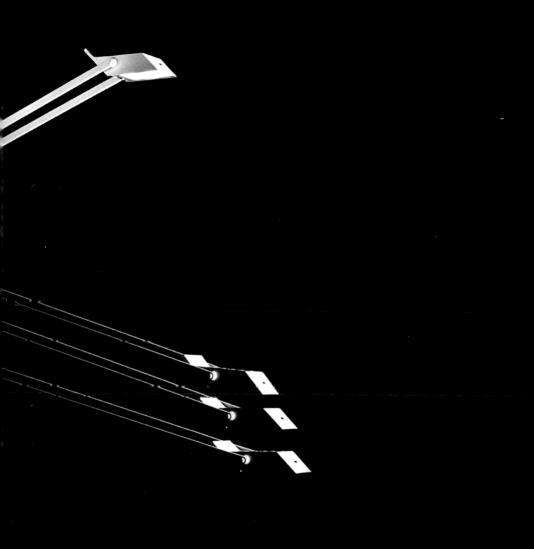

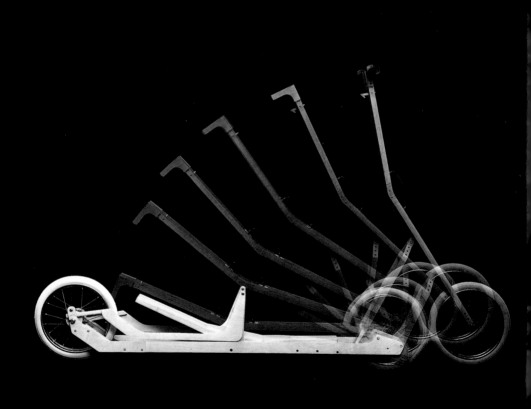

FOLDING SCOOTER PROTOTYPE, 1979

EXPERIMENTAL BIKE TRAFFIC STUDY FOR MILAN, CONDUCTED WITH GAE AULENTI, 1972

FOLDING BICYCLE FOR BATAVUS, 1976

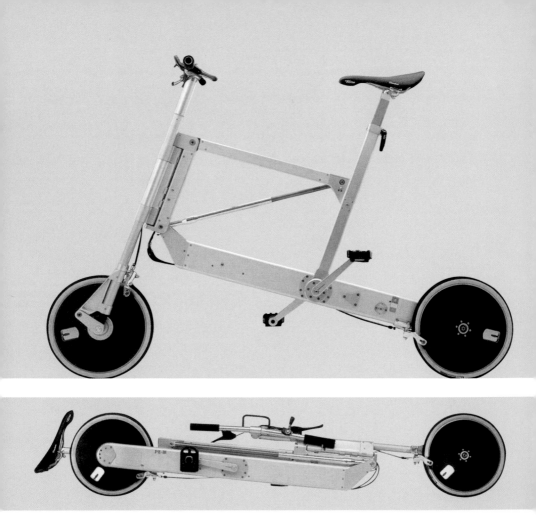

"I wanted to invent a bicycle that had all the conventional features, but could be folded as quickly as an umbrella, and would be small enough to fit in the trunk of car or a closet at home. I thought: What if the bicycle had not been invented, and I could design one with the same advanced technology as an aircraft's landing gear? I tried it and found I could."

ZOOMBIKE FOLDING BICYCLE FOR
ELETTROMONTAGGI, 2000

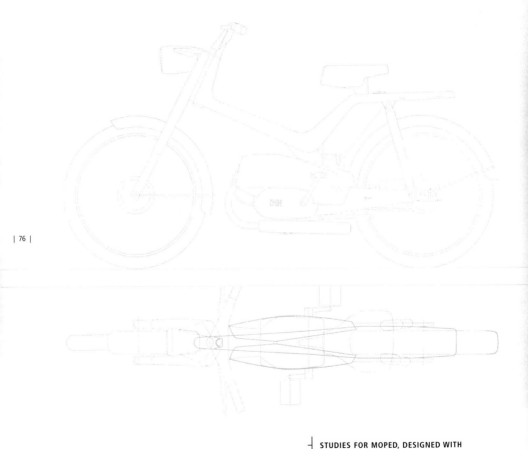

STUDIES FOR MOPED, DESIGNED WITH
ALBERTO ROSELLI, 1958

CAR BODY MODEL FOR TOURING (MILAN), 1968

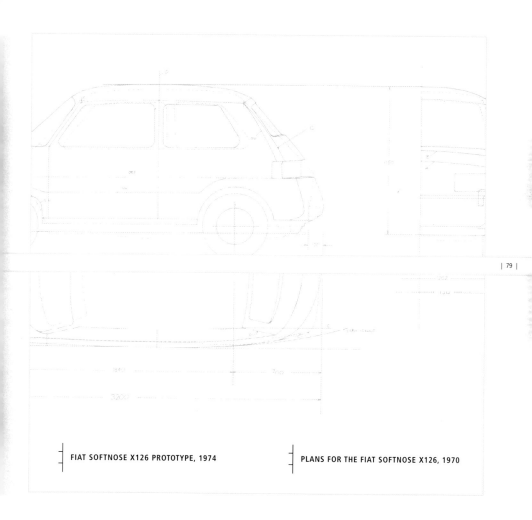

FIAT SOFTNOSE X126 PROTOTYPE, 1974

PLANS FOR THE FIAT SOFTNOSE X126, 1970

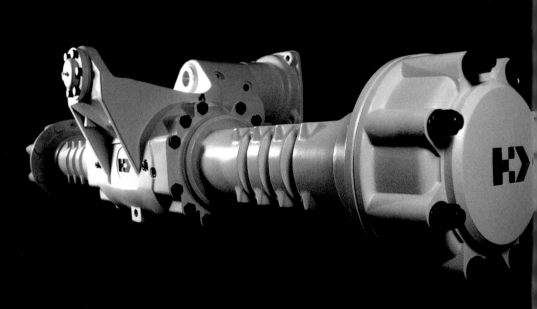

In an era of computer-generated blobs and squishy, multicolored, "user-friendly" shapes, Sapper swims against the tide. He finds a timeless beauty in minimal, monochromatic, orthogonal forms. It is his invisible signature, one that adds value to the product. More than ten million ThinkPads have been sold, and research has determined that up to a third were chosen primarily for their appearance.

POWER TRANSMISSION SYSTEM FOR
HURTH-AXLE, 1990

DONEY 14 TELEVISION, DESIGNED WITH MARCO
ZANUSO, FOR BRIONVEGA, 1962

ROCKET ELECTRONIC DIGITAL DESK CLOCK FOR
RITZ-ITALORA, 1971

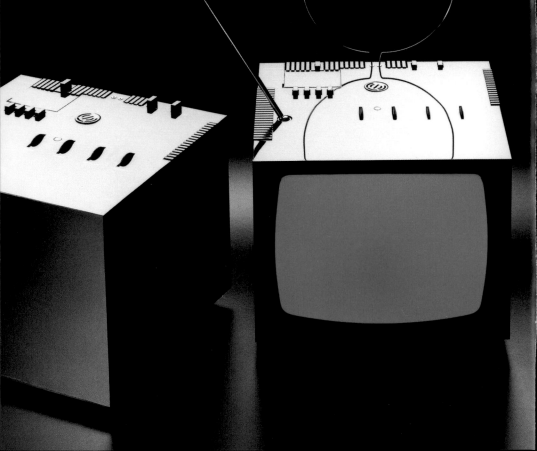

BLACK TV, DESIGNED WITH MARCO ZANUSO,
FOR BRIONVEGA, 1969

ALGOL TELEVISION TVC 11 FOR BRIONVEGA,
1985; IN BACKGROUND: ALGOL TELEVISION,
DESIGNED WITH MARCO ZANUSO, 1962–64

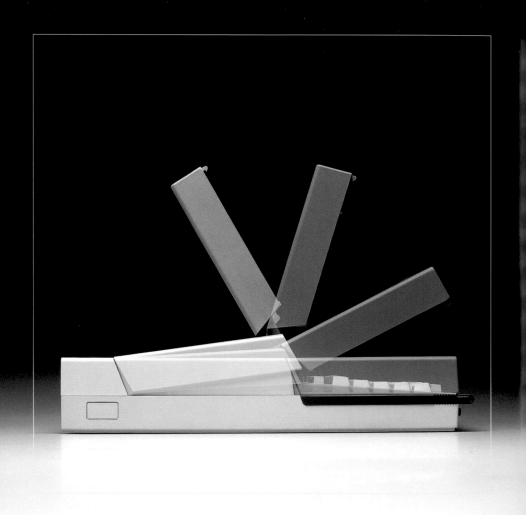

5140 CONVERTIBLE PC FOR IBM, 1985

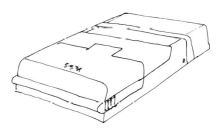

PS/2N33SX NOTEBOOK-COMPUTER, DESIGNED
WITH KAZUHIKO YAMAZAKI, FOR IBM, 1992

THINKPAD 570 ENGAGING WITH ITS DOCKING STATION, DESIGNED WITH KAZUHIKO YAMAZAKI, TOMOYUKI TAKAHASHI, AND DAVID HILL, FOR IBM, 1999

INSET PHOTO: THINKPAD 240, DESIGNED WITH KAZUHIKO YAMAZAKI, NARIAKI MIEKI, AND DAVID HILL, FOR IBM, 1999

LEAPFROG PROTOTYPE WORKSTATION, DESIGNED
WITH SAM LUCENTE, FOR IBM, 1992

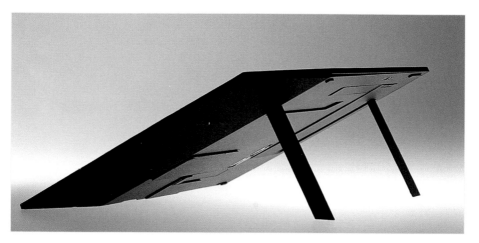

NETVISTA X40 PC, DESIGNED WITH KATE WALKER,
DAVID HILL, JOHN SWANSEY, BRIAN LEONARD,
TONY LATTO, AND BOB SPRINGER, FOR IBM, 2000

FOLLOWING PAGE: RICHARD SAPPER, 1999

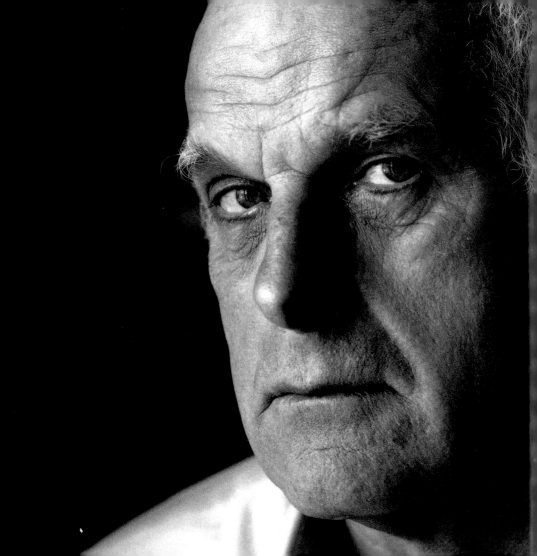

RICHARD SAPPER BIOGRAPHY

1932   Born in Munich, Germany; his family moves shortly thereafter to Stuttgart, where he spends most of his childhood

1956   Graduates from the University of Munich with a graduate degree in business administration; goes to work in the styling department of Daimler-Benz

1958   Moves to Milan where he works as a designer first for Gio Ponti, and then La Rinascente department store

1959   While continuing to work on independent design projects, begins to collaborate on projects with Marco Zanuso; their partnership will last more than 15 years. Co-edits the Italian edition of a monograph on Paul Klee with Mario Spagnol. Wins the Compasso d'Oro, Italy's most prestigious design prize, for Lorenz's Static table clock.

1968   Organizes an exhibition on the boundaries of technology for the XIV Triennale in cooperation with Pio Mànzu and William Lansing Plumb

1970–76   Consults for Fiat on the design of experimental automobiles and for Pirelli on pneumatic structures

1971   Designs with Marco Zanuso a transportable living unit for the exhibition "Italy: the New Domestic Landscape" at the Museum of Modern Art (MoMA), New York

1972   Forms with Gae Aulenti a study group to explore solutions for inner-city traffic congestion, a topic he developed further for the XVI Triennale. Artemide introduces his Tizio lamp; some 1.5 million have since been sold.

1980   Succeeds the fabled Eliot Noyes as corporate industrial design consultant for IBM, a position which entails supervising the design of its products worldwide

        Sapper has taught and lectured in Vienna, Stuttgart, Milan, London, Beijing, and Buenos Aires. His products have won the Compasso d'Oro ten times, and more than 15 of his designs are in MoMA's permanent design collection.

INDEX